From C to Shining C

From Cancer to Christ

A Devotional for the Journey of Cancer

S. JUDE PEREGRINE

WESTBOW
PRESS®
A DIVISION OF THOMAS NELSON
& ZONDERVAN

WestBow Press books may be ordered through booksellers or by contacting:

WestBow Press
A Division of Thomas Nelson & Zondervan
1663 Liberty Drive
Bloomington, IN 47403
www.westbowpress.com
1 (866) 928-1240

ISBN: 978-1-5127-3388-4 (sc)
ISBN: 978-1-5127-3389-1 (hc)
ISBN: 978-1-5127-3387-7 (e)

Library of Congress Control Number: 2016903924

Print information available on the last page.

WestBow Press rev. date: 10/5/2016

Table of Contents

Dedication

This book is dedicated and written in honor of St. Jude, St. Peregrine, Blessed Mother Mary, and God the Father, God the Son and the Holy Spirit.

I also want to thank and acknowledge the many people who supported me on my journey from cancer to Christ.

To my husband and best friend, you cared for me through this journey and I love and admire your strength and commitment.

To my wonderful neighbors in Chase Farms and Cindy T. Thank you for stepping in to fill the gap and lightening the burden for my family. You are all gracious and loving women.

To my parents. Thank you for dedicating yourselves to me during this journey. I know it was difficult.

To Rose, my cousin and best friend. Thank you for listening, uplifting me and for being there when I needed you the most.

To my dear friend Vira, this book could never have been completed without your dedication and the hundreds of hours you invested.

To Father John Buddee, Father John Riccardo, and Father Joe Horn. Thank you for praying with me, and graciously and patiently listening to my confessions and questions.

To Jack Krasula and Raye LaPlante. Thank you for providing financial, emotional and mental support for me and my family.

To Dr. R. Pariakh, Dr. D. Ruark, and Dr. F. Vincini for giving so much more than medical expertise and advice.

These are just a few of the amazing people who walked along side of me as I journeyed from cancer to Christ.

Acknowledgements

Many people gave generously of their time and energy to bring this book into being. Their contributions are woven into the words on every page.

I would like to acknowledge my dear friend and colleague Vira, for she gave generously of her time. Vira's encouragement, research and organization skills were instrumental in the development of this book.

I am grateful to have benefited from the skillful and talented editor Linette Wheeler who graciously gave of her time and talent.

I am grateful to Father Norman Fischer for the front and back book cover design and for the images that appear within the book.

I am grateful to the individuals that reviewed the manuscript, Teresa, Rose, Josephine, Vira, Paul, Scott, and Lorena.

Foreword

"I've got cancer!"

I can remember the phone call from a close friend like it was this morning. Few words have a grip on us like that word: cancer. It brings the entire gamut of emotions: disbelief, dread, anxiety, anger, and so much more. Unfortunately, many of us do in fact receive the news from our doctor that we have it. If you're reading this now, then that conversation has already taken place and either someone who loves you has given you S. Jude's book or you have purchased it yourself. I would simply say two things at the outset. First, this is an invaluable tool, written from the perspective of someone who has been where you are right now and is able to walk with you every step of the way. I will be handing this Devotional out in mass quantities, as S. Jude not only gets it, but she keeps our eyes forward on a most important truth. That truth is the second thing I'd like to say: you are, right now, at this moment, as you read these words, not in the hands of a disease, nor even the hands of your doctors and nurses, skilled and loving as they are; you are in the hands of your Heavenly Father who loves you, who sent His only Begotten Son into the world for you, who is never nervous or anxious. And right now, at this moment, as you read these words, He wants you to hear His voice whispering to you in your heart: "You're my daughter," or "You're my son." Do not be afraid.

Father John Riccardo
"Christ is the Answer" Ave Maria Radio
Pastor at Our Lady of Good Counsel in Plymouth, Michigan

Preface

This devotional is meant to be a guide that accompanies you on the journey of cancer. Cancer is so much more than just a physical illness. It has mental, emotional, and spiritual components. Although it may be hard to imagine right now, one day you will see and even be thankful for this journey. The ordeal of cancer strengthens you and your perception of life. If you allow it, this journey will positively change how you see and experience everything because it creates the opportunity to reorganize your life and rediscover what is really important to you. Challenges that would have caused grief in the past no longer bear the same sting, because you know what really matters. You truly learn to appreciate that the best things in life are truly free. The love for your family and friends will become stronger and deeper. Your relationship and faith in God will become the foundation on which everything else is built. Although you would never choose this journey for yourself or wish it upon anyone, you will come to realize that this journey is a unique gift that gives more than it takes.

This book is meant to be your personal devotional during your journey. Each chapter contains four sections:

- The first section is a **Reflection**. The reflections describe the emotions and thoughts experienced by many that have been on the journey of cancer.
- The second section is the **Word of God**. The Bible verses are specific to the emotions and thoughts expressed in the reflection.
- The third section is a **Prayer**. The prayers take many forms. In some instances they are a conversation between you and God or

prayers from the heart. In other instances the prayers are well known prayers such as "Hail Mary."

- The fourth and last section is open space for you to document your **reflections, thoughts, and emotions.**

Each chapter is self-contained and independent of the other chapters so you can use it chronologically or, if you choose, you can jump around to chapters that address a specific emotion or need.

In the Appendix, there is a series of prayers and novenas to support you during your journey.

May God the Father, God the Son and the Holy Spirit bless you and give you peace and strength as you travel the journey of cancer. I pray for your physical, emotional, mental, and spiritual healing and restoration. Amen.

Chapter 1
The World Stops

The world has stopped just like it did on September 11, 2001, the day the United States of America was attacked with our own commercial airlines. But when the world stops this time, it is less newsworthy but certainly much more personal. You go to the doctor for what you believe to be a standard visit to diagnose what you expect to be an infection, a pulled muscle, or something uneventful, and the doctor shares her concern of cancer. Just like that, your world stops!

You think, *"This cannot be right. I feel good. The next test will show there is no cancer."*

Word of God   2 Corinthians 4:17–18

For this momentary light affliction is producing for us an eternal weight of glory beyond all comparison, as we look not to what is seen but to what is unseen; for what is seen is transitory, but what is unseen is eternal.

Word of God   Job 12:10

In his hand is the soul of every living thing, and the life breath of all mortal flesh.

Word of God   Psalm 25:1–3

To you, O LORD, I lift up my soul, my God, in you I trust; do not let me be disgraced; do not let my enemies gloat over me. No one is disgraced who waits for you.

Word of God   Romans 12:12

Rejoice in hope, endure in affliction, persevere in prayer.

Prayer

Jesus, I beg you that the next test will show there is no cancer. Please Lord. I am here on my knees, and I beg you to have all tests show that my cells are normal and healthy. I will do anything for you Lord. Please do this for me. Amen.

Write Down Your Reflections and Feelings:

Chapter 2

Am I Being Punished?

God! Are you punishing me? What did I do to deserve this? Nothing is as I thought it was. God, you are not as I thought you were. Why are you punishing me?

Word of God   1 Peter 5:7, 10

Cast all your worries upon him because he cares for you. The God of all grace who called you to his eternal glory through Christ will himself restore, confirm, strengthen, and establish you after you have suffered a little.

Word of God   2 Chronicles 30:9

The LORD, your God, is gracious and merciful and he will not turn away his face from you.

Word of God   Isaiah 63:15–16

LORD, where is your zealous care and your might, your surge of pity? Your mercy hold not back! ... You, LORD, are our father, our redeemer.

*Y*ou, LORD, are a compassionate and gracious God, slow to anger, abounding in mercy and truth. Turn to me, be gracious to me; give your strength to your servant.

Prayer

Jesus, are you punishing me? I am a good person. I go to church every Sunday. Lord, be merciful toward me. Please God, heal me. Take this illness from me. Mary, my mother, I need you. Please ask your Son to heal me. Why are you punishing me? I know you can heal me so please heal me. I beg you to do this for me. Amen.

Write Down Your Reflections and Feelings:

Chapter 3

Fear

I am so afraid. My mind is racing with "what if's." I cannot sleep, eat, or hold a normal conversation. There is so much angst. I have always been able to control and influence outcomes, but this I cannot influence. This is beyond me.

Word of God   Isaiah 35:4

Say to the fearful of heart: Be strong, do not fear! Here is your God, he comes with vindication.

Word of God   Jeremiah 29:11–12

For I know well the plans I have in mind for you ... plans for your welfare and not for woe, so as to give you a future of hope. When you call me, and come and pray to me, I will listen to you.

Word of God   2 Timothy 1:7

God did not give us a spirit of cowardice but rather of power and love and self-control.

Word of God   Matthew 10:31

o not be afraid.

Word of God   Psalm 56:4–5

When I am afraid, in you I place my trust. I praise the word of God; I trust in God, I do not fear.

Word of God   Romans 8:15

For you did not receive a spirit of slavery to fall back into fear, but you received a spirit of adoption, through which we cry, "Abba, Father!" The Spirit itself bears witness with our spirit that we are children of God.

Prayer

Father, your Word says to let not my heart be troubled, neither let it be afraid. Father God, I need your help for I am so afraid. God help me. Give me peace. Comfort me so I can enjoy this day. Amen.

Write Down Your Reflections and Feelings:

Chapter 4

I Am Desperate

The diagnoses and tests never seem to end. I am desperate. I want to share my thoughts and fears, but yet I am afraid. What will people think of me if I tell them how fearful and desperate I am? I am alone.

Word of God   Lamentations 2:18

Cry out to the LORD from your heart, wall of daughter Zion! Let your tears flow like a torrent day and night.

Word of God   Isaiah 54:10

Though the mountains fall away and the hills be shaken, My love shall never fall away from you nor my covenant of peace be shaken, says the LORD.

Word of God   Sirach 51:7–10

I turned every way, but there was no one to help; I looked for support but there was none. Then I remembered the mercies of the LORD, his acts of kindness through ages past; For he saves those who take refuge in him, and rescues them from every evil. So ... I cried for help. I called out: LORD, you are my Father, my champion, my savior! Do not abandon me in time of trouble, in the midst of storms and dangers.

Word of God

Psalm 130:1–2

O ut of the depths I call to you, LORD; LORD, hear my cry! May your ears be attentive to my cry for mercy.

Word of God

Psalm 31:2

I n you, LORD, I take refuge; let me never be put to shame. In your righteousness deliver me.

Prayer

O protector and guardian angel assigned to me by the Creator, I ask for your unfailing intercession to petition the blessings I am in greatest need of from God the Father, God the Son, and the Holy Spirit. I place my confident trust in you and ask for peace for my heart and mind. Hold me close and protect me from fear and desperation.

Mother Mary, you are the mother of Jesus and my mother, I ask for your grace of peace. Please present my petition to your divine Son, Jesus, for the blessings you know that I need. Amen.

Write Down Your Reflections and Feelings:

Chapter 5

Anguish

This journey of cancer not only brings me anguish but it also brings anguish to dozens of others: my spouse, my parents, my children, my friends, my work colleagues, my brothers and sisters, and even the doctors. Everyone shares in this anguish.

Word of God   Psalm 25:17–18

Relieve the troubles of my heart; bring me out of my distress. Look upon my affliction and suffering; take away all my sins.

Word of God   Romans 12:4, 5, 15, 16

For as in one body we have many [members] ... so we, though many, are one body in Christ ... Rejoice with those who rejoice, weep with those who weep. Have the same regard for one another.

Word of God   1 Thessalonians 5:11

Encourage one another and build one another up, as indeed you do.

Blessed be the God and Father of our LORD Jesus Christ, the Father of compassion and God of all encouragement, who encourages us in our every affliction, so that we may be able to encourage those who are in any affliction with the encouragement with which we ourselves are encouraged by God.

Prayer

Dear God, my spouse, parents, and children are suffering along with me. Father God, I ask you to bless and keep my spouse, parents, children, and *(mention those whom you would like to pray for)*. Let your face shine upon them and be gracious to them. Please look kindly upon them and give them peace. Amen.

Write Down Your Reflections and Feelings:

Chapter 6

Each Decision I Make
Is So Important

So much information to absorb and so many decisions to make. Are these the right doctors? Is this the right treatment plan? There is so much riding on these decisions. Each one is so important. I pray for guidance.

Word of God   Proverbs 20:18

Plans made with advice succeed.

Word of God   Psalm 32:8

I will instruct you and show you the way you should walk, give you counsel with my eye upon you.

Word of God   Matthew 7:7–12

Ask and it will be given to you; seek and you will find; knock and the door will be opened to you. For everyone who asks, receives; and the one who seeks, finds; and to the one who knocks, the door will be opened. Which one of you would hand his son a stone when he asks for a loaf of bread, or a snake when he asks for a fish? If you then, who are wicked, know how to give good gifts to your children, how much more will your heavenly Father give good things to those who ask him.

Word of God   Isaiah 42:16

I **will lead** the blind on a way they do not know; by paths they do not know I will guide them ... These are my promises: I made them, I will not forsake them.

Word of God   Deuteronomy 14:29

So that the LORD, your God, may bless you in all that you undertake.

Word of God   Jeremiah 42:3

Let the LORD God show us what way we should take and what we should do.

Prayer

God, you know all things. You know when I sit and when I stand. You know how many hairs are on my head. Reveal to me the treatment plan and doctors to work with. My life is in your hands. Show me the way.

Our Father who art in heaven, hallowed be your name, your kingdom come, your will be done on earth as it is in heaven. Give me this day my daily bread, and forgive me my trespasses as I forgive those who have trespassed against me. Lead me not into temptation but deliver me from all evil. Deliver me Lord from illness into perfect health. I ask this in the name of Jesus and through the immaculate heart of my Mother Mary. Amen.

Write Down Your Reflections and Feelings:

Prayer

Chapter 7

Why?

My mind races with thoughts of *"why and how did this happen?"* Was this caused by my diet? Was it something I ate? Did I cause this? Could this be caused by something I cannot see?

Word of God   2 Kings 20:5

I have heard your prayer; I have seen your tears. Now I am healing you.

Word of God   Psalm 107:1, 17, 19–22

Give thanks to the LORD for he is good; for his mercy endures forever! Some fell sick from their wicked ways, afflicted because of their sins. In their distress they cried to the LORD, who saved them in their peril, Sent forth his word to heal them, and snatched them from the grave. Let them thank the LORD for his mercy, such wondrous deeds for the children of Adam. Let them offer a sacrifice in thanks, recount his works with shouts of joy.

Prayer

Father, I do not know why this has happened, but I ask you to heal me and carry me through this. Give me the wisdom, discernment, and strength to endure what I must endure.

Glory be to the Father, the Son, and the Holy Spirit. As it was in the beginning, is now and ever shall be, now and forever. Amen.

Write Down Your Reflections and Feelings:

Chapter 8

I Want My Life Back

Test after test, doctor appointment after doctor appointment. Enough! When can this be over? When can I get my life back? Everyone else is laughing and having fun while I am suffering over test results. Everyone else is living their lives while my life is on hold. I want my old life back.

(Dear Reader, Your life will never be the same after this journey and although it may be difficult to believe now, it will be even better. One day you will be thankful for this journey and at the same time you will never want to go through this again.)

Word of God   1 Peter 1:6–7

Rejoice, although now for a little while you may have to suffer through various trials, so that the genuineness of your faith, more precious than gold that is perishable even though tested by fire, may prove to be for praise, glory, and honor ... of Jesus Christ.

Word of God   1 Corinthians 10:13

God is faithful and will not let you be tried beyond your strength; but with the trial he will also provide a way out, so that you may be able to bear it.

Prayer

God, you have given me a wonderful family and wonderful friends. I cannot believe you want to take me away from all of this. I miss my old life. I miss laughing and having fun. Why can't I have my old life back? I long for my old worries and troubles. God, please give me back what I had. Heal me, restore my life. Please, I beg you God. Amen.

Write Down Your Reflections and Feelings:

Chapter 9

What Do I Tell People?

People are asking me about the illness and I do not know what to say because their reactions affect me negatively. Some people ask penetrating questions and want details, while others tell stories of people they know that have had cancer. They mean well, but often their words and reactions are difficult to bear. I feel they are asking for their own reasons, and wondering if and how they can prevent something like this from happening to them.

What do I tell people? I do not want to talk about the details of the diagnosis. Instead, I ask them to pray for my healing in mind, body, and spirit.

Word of God   Mark 2:1–5, 10–12

When Jesus returned to Capernaum after some days, it became known that he was at home. Many gathered together so that there was no longer room for them, not even around the door, and he preached the word to them. They came bringing to him a paralytic carried by four men. Unable to get near Jesus because of the crowd, they opened up the roof above him. After they had broken through, they let down the mat on which the paralytic was lying. **When Jesus saw their faith**, he said to the paralytic, "Child, your sins are forgiven. But that you may know that the Son of Man has authority to forgive sins on earth" – he said to the paralytic, "I say to you, rise, pick up your mat, and go home." He rose, picked up his mat at once, and went away in the sight of everyone. They were all astounded and glorified God, saying, "We have never seen anything like this."

Word of God   Jeremiah 17:14

Heal me **LORD**, that I may be healed; save me, that I may be saved, for you are my praise.

Word of God   Mark 1:40

If **you wish** [LORD], you can make me clean.

Prayer

Father God, Jesus, Holy Spirit, in the gospel of the paralytic man, it was not the paralytic man's faith but his friend's faith that caused his healing. You have blessed me with wonderful friends and family. Please hear their prayers, along with my own, to heal me. Please give me the words to speak when I am asked about my health. Thank you Father, Son, and Holy Spirit. Amen.

Write Down Your Reflections and Feelings:

Chapter 10

I Am Angry With You God

God! Is this love? Is this goodness and kindness? I am angry with you. I'm not a bad person. I don't abuse or kill people. I don't cheat or steal from others. I am a good person! I don't deserve this. God, you are in control. Why did you let this happen to me?

(Dear Reader, God knows your deepest thoughts so do not pretend and hide your true feelings from him. If you are angry with the Creator, express it. Tell God, because he already knows it. He wants an honest and open relationship with you. You are his precious creation.)

Word of God   Psalm 139:1–2

Lord ... you understand my thoughts from afar.

Word of God   Psalm 139:4

Even before a word is on my tongue, LORD, you know it all.

Word of God   Psalm 139:23(KJV)

Search me, O God ... know my thoughts.

Prayer

Jesus, why are you letting this happen to me? I have begged you to heal me and yet things are not getting better. I don't understand why I have to go through this. I want to live. Are you listening to me? Heal me, God. I know you can. Amen.

Hail Mary, full of grace. The Lord is with you. Blessed are you among women and blessed is the fruit of your womb, Jesus. Hail Mary, Mother of God, pray for me. Amen.

Write Down Your Reflections and Feelings:

Chapter 11

A New Honest Beginning

It is so strange that I feel better after yelling and fighting with God. This is the first time I have been totally honest and open with God. God wants complete openness. He knows me better than I know myself. He does not want me to hold back on what I think and feel. He wants me to come to him with all my cares and worries. He wants all of it, the good, the bad, and the ugly so he can transform it into peace.

Word of God   Psalm 139:1–6, 13–18

LORD, you have probed me, you know me: you know when I sit and stand, you understand my thoughts from afar. You sift through my travels and my rest; with all my ways you are familiar. Even before a word is on my tongue, LORD, you know it all. Behind and before you encircle me and rest your hand upon me. Such knowledge is too wonderful for me, far too lofty for me to reach. You formed my inmost being; you knit me in my mother's womb. I praise you, because I am wonderfully made; wonderful are your

23

works! My very self you know. My bones are not hidden from you, When I was being made in secret, fashioned in the depths of the earth. Your eyes saw me unformed; in your book all are written down; my days were shaped, before one came to be. How precious to me are your designs, O God; how vast the sum of them! Were I to count them, they would outnumber the sands; when I complete them, still you are with me.

Prayer

Good Morning God, thank you for this new sense of calmness and peace. You are gracious and merciful to me, even when I don't deserve it. Thank you God. Glory be to the Father, the Son, and the Holy Spirit. As it was in the beginning, is now and ever shall be, now and forever. Amen.

Write Down Your Reflections and Feelings:

Chapter 12

I Don't Want to
Lose My Hair

This journey of cancer is hard. It strips me down to nothing, both internally
and externally. I won't even look like myself. I don't want to lose my hair.
My appearance has always been important to me. I don't want to lose my
looks. There is just so much to deal with.

Word of God   Proverbs 31:30(KJV)

Favour is deceitful, and beauty is vain: but a woman that feareth
the LORD, she shall be praised.

Word of God   Proverbs 31:10(KJV)

Who can find a virtuous woman? for her price is far above
rubies.

Word of God   1 Samuel 16:7

God does not see as a mortal, who sees the appearance. The
LORD looks into the heart.

Prayer

Father God, I come before you now and I want to be beautiful on the inside. I pray for a new, clean, beautiful heart. I have sinned with my thoughts and with my words, and by what I have done and what I have failed to do. I ask for forgiveness. I ask for a new loving heart that is sensitive to sin. Please wash my mind, heart, and body clean in Jesus' precious blood. Please make them new and beautiful. I ask this in Jesus' name and through the immaculate heart of Mary. Amen.

Write Down Your Reflections and Feelings:

Chapter 13

What Does My Heart Look Like?

I want to be beautiful on the inside. What does my heart look like? I wonder what God sees in my heart? Is it beautiful? Is it soft and tender? Often I speak words that are not loving or kind. It is so hard to examine my heart and think about what it looks like to God. I do not want to think about this, but yet if I truly seek healing I must be brave and take this step.

Word of God   Matthew 12:34(KJV)

For out of the abundance of the heart the mouth speaketh.

Word of God   Leviticus 19:17–18

You shall not hate any of your kindred in your heart. Reprove your neighbor openly so that you do not incur sin because of that person. Take no revenge and cherish no grudge against your own people. You shall love your neighbor as yourself.

Word of God   Jeremiah 17:14

Heal me, LORD, that I may be healed; save me, that I may be saved, for you are my praise.

Word of God   Mark 7:20–22

But what comes out of a person, that is what defiles. From within people, from their hearts, come evil thoughts, unchastity, theft, murder, adultery, greed, malice, deceit, licentiousness, envy, blasphemy, arrogance, folly.

Word of God   Proverbs 31:25(ASV)

Strength and dignity are her clothing.

Word of God   Ephesians 4:26–27, 31

Do not sin; do not let the sun set on your anger, and do not leave room for the devil. All bitterness, fury, anger, shouting, and reviling must be removed from you, along with all malice.

Prayer

Father God, I now see that hatred, anger, and unforgiveness cause my heart to be hard and ugly to you. I see that my sins tend to be sins of the heart. Lord give me a new heart that is loving and kind. A heart that honors you. Relieve anguish from my heart and free me from my past and wrong thinking. Amen.

Write Down Your Reflections and Feelings:

Chapter 14
Beginning To Make A Beautiful Heart

I now understand that hatred, anger, and unforgiveness create a heart that is ugly to God. I want a soft and loving heart. I want God to find my heart beautiful. I need to forgive those who have hurt me. I also need to forgive myself for all the mistakes I have made. A beautiful heart begins by forgiving.

Word of God   Ephesians 4:31–32

All **bitterness**, fury, anger, shouting, and reviling must be removed from you, along with all malice. [And] be kind to one another, compassionate, forgiving one another as God has forgiven you in Christ.

Word of God   Galatians 5:22–23(ASV)

The fruit of the Spirit is love, joy, peace, longsuffering, kindness, goodness, faithfulness, meekness, self-control.

Word of God   Matthew 6:9–12(KJV)

[Pray in] this manner ... Our Father which art in heaven, Hallowed be thy name. Thy kingdom come, Thy will be done in earth, as it is in heaven. Give us this day our daily bread. And forgive us our debts, as we forgive our debtors.

Word of God   Luke 6:28(KJV)

Bless them that curse you, and pray for them which despitefully use you.

Word of God   Psalm 51:10(KJV)

Create in me a clean heart, O God; and renew a right spirit within me.

Prayer

Jesus, through the power of the Holy Spirit, please heal me physically, spiritually, and emotionally. Holy Spirit, go back in my memory and heal every hurt that has been done to me. Please Holy Spirit, be Lord of my heart and heal every hurt I have ever caused to another person. Heal all the relationships that I have damaged in my whole life.

Holy Spirit, is there anything that I need to do? Do I need to go to a person because he/she is still suffering from my words or actions? If so, bring that person to my awareness so I can go to them and ask for forgiveness. I choose to forgive, and I ask to be forgiven. Remove any bitterness, hatred,

30

anger, jealousy, and unforgiveness from my heart and fill all those empty spaces with Jesus' pure perfect love.

Thank you Father, Son, and Holy Spirit. Amen.

Write Down Your Reflections and Feelings:

Chapter 15

Forgiveness Is A Journey Not An Event

Purifying my heart is a journey that I want and need to pursue. I need to rid myself of the burden of unforgiveness and sin by asking God for forgiveness, and asking forgiveness from those that I have hurt or wronged.

Word of God   Hebrews 12:1–2

Let us rid ourselves of every burden and sin that clings to us and persevere in running the race that lies before us while keeping our eyes fixed on Jesus.

Word of God   Ephesians 4:31–32

All bitterness, fury, anger, shouting, and reviling must be removed from you, along with all malice. [And] be kind to one another, compassionate, forgiving one another as God has forgiven you in Christ.

Word of God   Ephesians 4:1–2

Live in a manner worthy of the call you have received, with all humility and gentleness, with patience, bearing with one another through love.

S earch me, O God ... know my thoughts: And see if there be any wicked way in me, and lead me in the way everlasting.

Prayer

Almighty God, I confess to you that I have sinned through my own fault. I have sinned in my thoughts and in my words. I have sinned in my heart. I have sinned in what I have done, and in what I have failed to do.

I ask for forgiveness and pray for a soft, loving heart where unforgiveness has no place to rest. Please Lord, show me where there is unforgiveness in my heart. Please give me a new, warm, soft heart that is honoring to you. Amen.

Write Down Your Reflections and Feelings:

Chapter 16

Faith Precedes Healing

Today is a good day and I feel better emotionally and physically. My emotional and physical wellness seem to be linked to forgiveness.

God is healing me physically, spiritually and emotionally. As the Bible reveals there is a strong connection between healing and faith. Day by day, and along every step of this difficult journey, my faith is growing and I am healing.

Word of God   Mark 5:25–34(KJV)

And a certain woman, which had an issue of blood twelve years, And had suffered many things of many physicians, and had spent all that she had, and was nothing bettered, but rather grew worse, When she had heard of Jesus, came in the press behind, and touched his garment. For she said, "If I may touch but his clothes, I shall be whole." And straightway the fountain of her blood was dried up; and she felt in her body that she was healed of that plague. And Jesus, immediately knowing in himself that virtue had gone out of him, turned him about in the press, and said, "Who touched my clothes?" And his disciples said unto him, "Thou seest the multitude thronging thee, and sayest thou, Who touched me?" And he looked round about to see her that had done this thing. But the woman fearing and trembling, knowing what was done in her, came and fell down before him, and told him all the truth. And he said unto her, "**Daughter, thy faith hath made thee whole**; go in peace, and be whole of thy plague."

Word of God   Mark 10:46–52(KJV)

And **they came to Jericho:** and as he went out of Jericho with his disciples and a great number of people, blind Bartimaeus, the son of Timaeus, sat by the highway side begging. And when he heard that it was Jesus of Nazareth, he began to cry out, and say, "Jesus, thou son of David, have mercy on me." And many charged him that he should hold his peace: but he cried the more a great deal, "Thou son of David, have mercy on me." And Jesus stood still, and commanded him to be called. And they called the blind man, saying unto him, "Be of good comfort, rise; he calleth thee." And he, casting away his garment, rose, and came to Jesus. And Jesus answered and said unto him, "What wilt thou that I should do unto thee?" The blind man said unto him, "LORD, that I might receive my sight." And Jesus said unto him, "Go thy way; **thy faith hath made thee whole.**" And immediately he received his sight, and followed Jesus in the way.

Word of God   Hebrews 11:1(KJV)

Now **faith** is the substance of things hoped for, the evidence of things not seen.

Word of God   Hebrews 11:6

But **without faith** it is impossible to please him, for anyone who approaches God must believe that he exists and that he rewards those who seek him.

Prayer

Jesus, you are Lord of this new day, and I proclaim you as Lord over all the senses of my body. You are Lord of all that I see, hear, speak, and love. I proclaim you Lord over my mind and every thought. You are Lord over my hands and all that I do, my feet and every step I take. You are Lord over every cell, tissue, and nerve ending in my body. You Jesus, are risen from the dead and I confess you as my Lord and God, now and forever. Amen.

Write Down Your Reflections and Feelings:

Chapter 17

The Days Of
Chemotherapy Are Here

Can I really do this? I don't know if I have it in me to take such a powerful medication. I don't want to sit in a room with sick people. I barely have the emotional strength, let alone the physical strength to endure this first treatment of chemotherapy.

I have prayed and prayed to be healed miraculously, but this is not God's plan for me and so this journey continues.

A Word from God

Be not afraid my sweet one. I will be there with you. I will hold you. Many people will seek their own agenda, but I am the only one who knows the future. You are safe in my arms. Pray upon your medicine so that it is strong against cancer but weak to all other cells.

Pray during the time you receive the medicine. It is time well spent. I will always be there to comfort you. Build a house in heaven that no one can tear down.

Word of God   Hebrews 12:2–3

While keeping our eyes fixed on Jesus, the leader and perfecter of faith. For the sake of the joy that lay before him he endured the cross, despising its shame, and has taken his seat at the right of the throne of God. Consider how he endured such opposition from sinners, in order that you may not grow weary and lose heart.

Word of God   Isaiah 12:2

God indeed is my salvation; I am confident and unafraid. For the LORD is my strength and my might.

Word of God   Hebrews 13:5–6

God has said, "I will never forsake you or abandon you." Thus we may say with confidence: "The LORD is my helper, [and] I will not be afraid. What can anyone do to me?"

Prayer

Father, Son, Holy Spirit, and my guardian angel, be by my side this day. Carry me for I cannot do this alone. I need your strength and peace to endure what must be endured. I ask this for myself and for all that are receiving chemotherapy this day. Amen.

Praying over the Medicine

Dear God, please bless this medicine and make it perfect for my health, energy, and healing. Make it strong against cancer and weak against the healthy cells. I ask this in the name of Jesus and through the immaculate heart of my Mother Mary. Amen.

Write Down Your Reflections and Feelings:

Chapter 18

So Much Fear, So Much Pain

Everyone else's world and lives seems to be moving forward while I suffer through this illness and miss all the fun.

(Dear Reader, The journey you are on is not meant to harm you. This is a journey which allows you to be restored to God if you allow it. God will help you. Call upon the Father, Jesus, and the Holy Spirit. They will help you carry this burden. Invite Jesus to carry this with you. There is nothing God would not do for you. God allowed the cancer but did not give it to you. Do not fear. God will never leave you. Speak to God. God is here and loves you.)

Word of God   Isaiah 40:31

They that hope in the LORD will renew their strength, they will soar as with eagles' wings; They will run and not grow weary, walk and not grow faint.

Word of God   Philippians 4:6–7

Have no anxiety at all, but in everything, by prayer and petition, with thanksgiving, make your requests known to God. Then the peace of God that surpasses all understanding will guard your hearts and minds in Christ Jesus.

Rejoice in hope, endure in affliction, persevere in prayer.

Prayer

In the name of Jesus, I come out of agreement with the spirit of fear. I proclaim Jesus Lord of my life, and I ask for the peace that can only come from you Jesus. I pray that the peace of the Lord rest upon me this day and forevermore. I ask this in the name of Jesus and through the immaculate heart of my loving Mother Mary. Amen.

Write Down Your Reflections and Feelings:

Chapter 19

Physical Health –
Spiritual Health

As I reflect upon my life, I now recognize the times when I chose to resist God. I recognize times when I chose to act out of love for myself, rather than act out of love for others or God. It is tough recognizing and realizing that I made every single one of those choices. I feel ashamed.

Word of God   Sirach 15:15–20

If you choose, you can keep the commandments; loyalty is doing the will of God. Set before you are fire and water; to whatever you choose, stretch out your hand. Before everyone are life and death, whichever they choose will be given them. Immense is the wisdom of the LORD; mighty in power, he sees all things. The eyes of God behold his works, and he understands every human deed. He never commands anyone to sin, nor shows leniency toward deceivers.

Word of God   Ecclesiastes 2:26

For to the one who pleases God, he gives wisdom and knowledge and joy; but to the one who displeases, God gives the task of gathering possessions for the one who pleases God. This also is vanity and a chase after wind.

Word of God   Proverbs 19:3

Their own folly leads people astray; in their hearts they rage against the LORD.

Word of God   Deuteronomy 8:6–7(KJV)

Therefore thou shalt keep the commandments of the LORD thy God, to walk in his ways, and to fear him. For the LORD thy God bringeth thee into a good land.

Word of God   1 John 1:5–10(KJV)

This then is the message which we have heard of him, and declare unto you, that God is light, and in him is no darkness at all. If we say that we have fellowship with him, and walk in darkness, we lie, and do not tell the truth: But if we walk in the light, as he is in the light, we have fellowship one with another, and the blood of Jesus Christ his Son cleanseth us from all sin. If we say that we have no sin, we deceive ourselves, and the truth is not in us. If we confess our sins, he is faithful and just to forgive us our sins, and to cleanse us from all unrighteousness. If we say that we have not sinned, we make him a liar, and his word is not in us.

Prayer

Dear Heavenly Father, help me to turn away from selfishness. I have strayed away from you Lord, physically, mentally, emotionally, and spiritually. Forgive my selfishness and reveal to me who you are. Guide me so that I am physically, mentally, emotionally, and spiritually healthy.

I want to bring you honor and glory through my words and my choices. Please forgive me where I have failed you in the past. I ask this in the name of Jesus and through the immaculate heart of my Mother Mary. Amen.

Write Down Your Reflections and Feelings:

Word of God   Jeremiah 2:11

Chapter 20

God Can Heal My Life

Although God has chosen not to heal me miraculously, I believe he is still healing me. The medicine works because he deems it to work. The healing I seek is more than physical. It is the healing of my life.

Word of God   Luke 6:19

Everyone in the crowd sought to touch him because power came forth from him and healed them all.

Word of God   Isaiah 57:18

I saw their ways, but I will heal them. I will lead them and restore full comfort to them.

Word of God   Hosea 14:5

I will heal their apostasy, I will love them freely.

Word of God   Jeremiah 30:17(KJV)

For I will restore health unto thee, and I will heal thee of thy wounds, saith the LORD.

For I know well the plans I have in mind for you ... plans for your welfare and not for woe, so as to give you a future of hope.

Prayer

God, you can do all things. You are the divine physician. You created me and you can heal me. I pray it is your will to heal my life so that I will be physically, emotionally, mentally, and spiritually healthy. I praise you Jesus, and I thank you Jesus. Amen.

Write Down Your Reflections and Feelings:

Chapter 21

Overcoming Fear

Today is a spiritual battle. I am afraid that if I give myself to God he will take me from Earth. I am afraid to surrender everything to God.

A Word from God

Precious Little One, there is no fear in love because love casts out all fear. Do not worry about the future or what you will wear for I will provide for you. You are suffering now but you shall live a life that is good and worthy. Do not be afraid for I will not harm you but will save you. Tomorrow is another day with new things to see. Rejoice and be not afraid.

Word of God   Psalm 23:4(KJV)

Though I walk through the valley of the shadow of death, I will fear no evil: for thou art with me; thy rod and thy staff they comfort me.

Word of God   Psalm 27:1(KJV)

The LORD is my light and my salvation; whom shall I fear? The LORD is the strength of my life; of whom shall I be afraid?

My soul rests in God alone, from whom comes my salvation. God alone is my rock and salvation, my fortress; I shall never fall.

Prayer

God, you know the fear that rages inside of me. You tell me in the Bible to "Not be afraid," and that you will not harm me. Ultimately this journey is in your hands. Ultimately I am in your hands. Please grant me a calmness and peace which surpasses all understanding. A peace that can only come from you. Amen.

Write Down Your Reflections and Feelings:

Chapter 22

Do Not Worry

My mind races with thoughts about the future and what the future holds. What if this happens? What if that occurs? I live from doctor appointment to doctor appointment, and test result to test result. I worry about what my future holds. I want to enjoy every moment with my family and live in the present.

Word of God   Matthew 6:25–30

Therefore I tell you, do not worry about your life, what you will eat, or about your body, what you will wear. Is not life more than food and the body more than clothing? Look at the birds in the sky; they do not sow or reap, they gather nothing into barns, yet your heavenly Father feeds them. Are not you more important than they? Can any of you by worrying add a single moment to your life-span? ... Learn from the way the wild flowers grow. They do not work or spin. But I tell you that not even Solomon in all his splendor was clothed like one of them. If God so clothes the grass of the field, which grows today and is thrown into the oven tomorrow, will he not much more provide for you?

Word of God   Matthew 6:34

Do not worry about tomorrow; tomorrow will take care of itself. Sufficient for a day is its own evil.

Word of God　　　　　　　　　　　　　　　　　Jeremiah 24:6(KJV)

For I will set mine eyes upon them for good ... and I will build them, and not pull them down.

Word of God　　　　　　　　　　　　　　　　　　　　Psalm 31:3–4

Be my rock of refuge, a stronghold to save me. For you are my rock and my fortress; for your name's sake lead me and guide me.

Prayer

Dear God the Father, God the Son, and Holy Spirit, I come to you full of worries, fears, and doubts about the future. Please calm my mind and grant me peace. Please replace anxiety with a peace that can only come from you. Give me the confidence to know that you are with me and will never leave me.

When I focus and dwell on past disappointments or hurts, open my mind to focusing on the present and the countless blessings that are in front of me right now. Release me from the hurts and pain of past experiences so I can enjoy each and every moment of this day. Lord, sometimes I cannot bear the stress and anxiety on my own. I ask you for grace and peace of mind and heart. Please fill me with faith, hope, peace and joy. Give me the strength to persevere. Renew me physically, spiritually, and emotionally. Fill me up with all that is good and holy. Amen.

Write Down Your Reflections and Feelings:

Chapter 23

Letting Go and Letting God

It is hard to grasp the realization that I do not have control and never really did have control over my life. In the past I believed I had control because I decided what events would fill my calendar. I decided with whom I would meet. I decided what I would do. All of this allowed me to believe that I was in control. This journey of cancer forces me to face the fact that my perception of control was just an illusion. I really have no control, only God is in control.

Word of God   1 Corinthians 2:9

What **eye has not seen,** and ear has not heard, and what has not entered the human heart, what God has prepared for those who love him.

Word of God　　　　　　　　　　　　　　**Colossians 1:16(KJV)**

For by him were all things created, that are in heaven, and that are in earth, visible and invisible ... all things were created by him, and for him.

Word of God　　　　　　　　　　　　　　**Proverbs 19:21**

Many are the plans of the human heart, but it is the decision of the LORD that endures.

Word of God　　　　　　　　　　　　　　**Romans 12:1–2**

I urge you therefore, brothers, by the mercies of God, to offer your bodies as a living sacrifice, holy and pleasing to God ... Do not conform yourselves to this age, but be transformed by the renewal of your mind.

Prayer

Dear God, I fear giving up control. I fear giving my whole self to you because that means giving up the comfortable perception of control. However, the truth is that I was never really in control. So now, in this moment, I invite you Jesus into my life as my Lord, God, and Savior. You are the one in control. Please keep me safe, heal me, change me, and strengthen me in body, soul, and spirit. Amen.

Write Down Your Reflections and Feelings:

Chapter 24

Can I Really Trust You God?

It is difficult to believe that God is trustworthy when all my experiences prove, time and time again, that <u>people</u> cannot be trusted. Every time I trust someone I am disappointed. Deep down, I know that I am not trustworthy. Given all these experiences, how do I learn to trust God? How do I trust that he loves me and wants the very best for me?

<u>Word of God</u>   Matthew 7:9, 11

Which one of you would hand his son a stone when he asks for a loaf of bread ... How much more will your heavenly Father give good things to those who ask Him.

<u>Word of God</u>   Isaiah 43:1–2

Do not fear, for I have redeemed you; I have called you by name: you are mine. When you pass through waters, I will be with you; through rivers, you shall not be swept away. When you walk through fire, you shall not be burned, nor will flames consume you.

<u>Word of God</u>   Luke 12:27–28

Notice how the flowers grow. They do not toil or spin. But I tell you, not even Solomon in all his splendor was dressed like one of them. If God so clothes the grass in the field ... will he not much more provide for you, O you of little faith?

With age-old love I have loved you; so I have kept my mercy toward you. Again I will build you, and you shall stay built.

Prayer

Dear Father, Son, and Holy Spirit, help my unbelief, support me and give me the opportunity to grow and succeed in learning to trust you. Please reveal yourself to me in a manner I can more fully understand your goodness, and your love for me. Help me to trust you, God. Amen.

Write Down Your Reflections and Feelings:

Chapter 25

God Is Not Human

Contemplating who God is and learning to trust Him is so foreign to me. I cannot apply my experiences with humans to God because God is not human. God is God. He is a being that is all knowing, all good, and always present. Out of the generosity of his heart, he chose to create me with the intent of sharing his love with me. He wants to know me. He so deeply wants to know me that he, the Creator, became one of the created in the person of Jesus.

Word of God   Hebrews 4:14–16

Therefore, since we have a great high priest who has passed through the heavens, Jesus, the Son of God, let us hold fast to our confession. For we do not have a high priest who is unable to sympathize with our weaknesses, but one who has similarly been tested in every way, yet without sin. So let us confidently approach the throne of grace to receive mercy and to find grace for timely help.

Word of God   Psalm 139:13–14

You formed my inmost being; you knit me in my mother's womb. I praise you, because I am wonderfully made; wonderful are your works! My very self you know.

Word of God   John 15:16(KJV)

Ye have not chosen me, but I have chosen you.

Word of God   John 15:12(KJV)

Love one another, as I have loved you.

Prayer

God my Father, God the Son, God the Holy Spirit, thank you for loving me when I have not always been lovable nor returned love to you. Forgive me for that. I want you and need you in my life. I want to know you the way you know me. I want to love you the way you love me. Mary, my mother in heaven, I ask you to be my guide to knowing, loving, and trusting your son, Jesus. Amen.

Write Down Your Reflections and Feelings:

Chapter 26

A Day Of Extremes

This journey of cancer is very spiritual. The questions I was too busy to contemplate face me now. Today has been a day of extremes. Initially, I felt extreme anguish because I feared surrendering to God fully and what would happen as a result of my surrender. But an inner voice is persistently and gently nudging me to let go and fully surrender to God. Finally, I fully surrender, and now I experience an extreme peace. Angst is replaced with a sense of calm.

Word of God   Luke 1:38

Behold, I am the handmaid of the LORD. May it be done to me according to your word.

Word of God   John 10:10

I came so that they might have life and have it more abundantly.

Word of God   Romans 12:1

I urge you therefore, brothers, by the mercies of God, to offer your bodies as a living sacrifice, holy and pleasing to God, your spiritual worship.

Word of God   Jeremiah 29:11

For I know well the plans I have in mind for you ... plans for your welfare and not for woe, so as to give you a future of hope.

Word of God   Psalm 25:17–18

Relieve the troubles of my heart; bring me out of my distress. Look upon my affliction and suffering; take away all my sins.

Word of God   Romans 6:13

Present yourselves to God ... and the parts of your bodies to God as weapons for righteousness.

Prayer

Lord Jesus, come into my heart. I desire that you be the Lord of my life. I desire to know you as my Savior. I open myself to receive you fully and without reservation. Thank you for bearing my sins. I believe in your forgiveness and ask you to forgive all of my sins. Take control of my life. Make me into the person you created me to be. I desire to never be separated from you and your everlasting love again. Thank you Father, Son, and Holy Spirit. Amen.

Write Down Your Reflections and Feelings:

Chapter 27

Peace

The anxiety has subsided. I feel peaceful. Thank you God, Jesus Christ, and Holy Spirit. I pray Lord, most gracious one, that it is your will that I will live and be healed.

Word of God   John 14:27(KJV)

Peace I leave with you, my peace I give unto you ... Let not your heart be troubled, neither let it be afraid.

Word of God   Matthew 11:28–30(KJV)

Come to me, all ye that labour and are heavy laden, and I will give you rest. Take my yoke upon you, and learn of me; for I am meek and lowly in heart: and ye shall find rest unto your souls. For my yoke is easy, and my burden is light.

The peace of God that surpasses all understanding, will guard your hearts and minds.

Prayer

Heavenly Father, thank you for granting me peace of mind and calming my troubled heart. Please continue to give me the strength and clarity of mind to grow in my love and knowledge of you and continue this journey.

Blessed Virgin Mary, Mother of God, pray for me. Thank you most Holy Trinity and Blessed Mother Mary. Amen.

Write Down Your Reflections and Feelings:

Chapter 28

Who And What Am I Worshipping?

At the beginning of this journey I never would have thought that I worshipped idols, but it is true, I did. God was probably in third or fourth place on my list of life's priorities. My list looked something like this: me, work, my kids, my husband, and then God. So who was I really worshipping? As painful and difficult as it is to admit, I was worshipping myself, first and foremost.

Word of God   Hosea 14:2

Return, Israel, to the LORD, your God.

Word of God   Psalm 81:9–10(KJV)

There shall no strange god be in thee; neither shalt thou worship any strange god. I am the LORD thy God, which brought thee out of the land of Egypt.

Word of God   Mark 12:30(KJV)

And thou shalt love the LORD thy God with all thy heart, and with all thy soul, and with all thy mind, and with all thy strength: this is the first commandment.

Thou shalt worship the LORD thy God, and him only shalt thou
serve.

Prayer

Forgive me Lord for placing things, myself, and other people in front of
you. I now understand that I was asking you to obey me, my wishes, my
commands. Please forgive my arrogance and conceit. I wish for you Jesus,
to be first in my life and to live according to your commands. Lord, I want
to be faithful to you. Thank you for being faithful to me. Amen.

Write Down Your Reflections and Feelings:

Chapter 29

Mercy

God loves me and wants the best for me. It is only because of his merciful grace that I now know this. I see that God knows everything about me, and in spite of all my faults and flaws he still desires me. I am loved.

Word of God   1 Peter 1:3

B lessed be the God and Father of our LORD Jesus Christ, who in his great mercy gave us a new birth to a living hope through the resurrection of Jesus Christ.

Word of God   Matthew 12:7

I desire mercy, not sacrifice.

Word of God   Psalm 51:3–4

H ave mercy on me, God, in accord with your merciful love; in your abundant compassion blot out my transgressions. Thoroughly wash away my guilt; and from my sin cleanse me.

Word of God   Hebrews 2:17–18

Therefore, [Christ] had to become like his brothers in every way, that he might be a merciful and faithful high priest before God to expiate the sins of the people. Because he himself was tested through what he suffered, he is able to help those who are being tested.

Word of God   Psalm 41:5

LORD, take note of me; heal me, although I have sinned against you.

Prayer

Dear Creator and Father, in you, mercy and love are endless and the treasury of compassion inexhaustible. Lord, look upon me kindly and increase your mercy in me so that in difficult moments I might not despair nor become despondent. You are my Father, and I submit myself to your holy will with confidence in heart and mind. Please grant me the graces of your love, mercy, and peace. Amen.

Pray the Chaplet of Divine Mercy.

Write Down Your Reflections and Feelings:

Chapter 30

Sin

This journey is forcing me to look at myself and the picture is not pretty. It is true that I have not killed anyone physically, but I have killed with my words and with my thoughts. My words and thoughts have been sinful. This sin has manifested in a physical, spiritual, and emotional illness. I now see that my thoughts and words have power to nurture and encourage a life, or injure and destroy a life. The choice is mine.

(Dear Reader, If you have not performed the Sacrament of Reconciliation recently, this is a wonderful and miraculous gift that leads to healing. If you do not remember how to do it, let the Catholic Priest know and he will kindly and gently walk you through it.)

Word of God   Mark 2:3–5

They came bringing to him a paralytic carried by four men. Unable to get near Jesus because of the crowd, they opened up the roof above him. After they had broken through, they let down the mat on which the paralytic was lying. When Jesus saw their faith, he said to paralytic, "Child, your sins are forgiven."

Word of God   Luke 6:37

Stop judging and you will not be judged. Stop condemning and you will not be condemned. Forgive and you will be forgiven.

Word of God   Hebrews 3:12

Take care, brothers, that none of you may have an evil and unfaithful heart, so as to forsake the living God. Encourage yourselves daily while it is still "today," so that none of you may grow hardened by the deceit of sin.

Word of God   Psalm 103:3–4, 8

Who pardons all your sins, and heals all your ills, Who redeems your life from the pit, and crowns you with mercy and compassion. Merciful and gracious is the LORD, slow to anger, abounding in mercy.

Prayer

Dear God, I confess to you that I have sinned in my thoughts and in my words. I have sinned in my actions, by what I have done, and what I have failed to do.

Look down upon me most good and gentle Jesus, while before Thy face I humbly kneel, and with burning soul plead you to restore deep in my heart a true sense of faith, hope, charity, and true contrition for my sins. I ask the Blessed Mary ever virgin, all the angels and saints to pray on my behalf to the Lord our God.

Almighty God, you are worthy of love and honor. I am truly sorry for sinning, because I know sinning is hurtful toward you. Please forgive my offenses and sins, and grant me the grace to begin anew, now, at this very moment. Amen.

Write Down Your Reflections and Feelings:

Chapter 31

Confession of Sin

One of the most difficult things to do is to verbalize and admit aloud my sins. For years I have asked to be forgiven for my sins in the silence and darkness, but stating my sins aloud is much more difficult. It is humiliating.

The reasons that make confessing my sins aloud so difficult are exactly the reasons I need to do it. Confessing aloud brings my sins into the light so they can be cleansed. Confession is not humiliating, it is demonstrating humility and acknowledging God.

Word of God   Isaiah 1:18–20(KJV)

Come now, and let us reason together, saith the LORD: though your sins be as scarlet, they shall be as white as snow; though they be red like crimson, they shall be as wool. If ye be willing and obedient, ye shall eat the good of the land: But if ye refuse and rebel, ye shall be devoured with the sword.

Word of God   Luke 15:18(KJV)

I will arise and go to my father, and will say unto him, Father, I have sinned against heaven, and before thee.

Word of God   Jeremiah 17:10

I the LORD, explore the mind and test the heart, Giving to all according to their ways, according to the fruit of their deeds.

Word of God   Psalm 32:1, 3, 5, 6

Blessed is the one whose fault is removed, whose sin is forgiven. Because I kept silent, my bones wasted away ... Then I declared my sin to you; my guilt I did not hide. I said, "I confess my transgression to the LORD," and you took away the guilt of my sin. Therefore every loyal person should pray to you in time of distress.

Word of God   Hebrews 4:14–16

Therefore, since we have a great high priest who has passed through the heavens, Jesus, the Son of God, let us hold fast to our confession. For we do not have a high priest who is unable to sympathize with our weaknesses, but one who has similarly been tested in every way, yet without sin. So let us confidently approach the throne of grace to receive mercy and to find grace for timely help.

Prayer

O Scared Heart of Jesus, you are the fountain of every blessing. I love you Jesus, and with a contrite heart and sorrow for my sins, I offer you myself fully: my mind, my heart, my body, and my soul. Transform me and make me humble, kind, loving, and obedient to you and your laws.

Lord, I wish for you to live in me, and I in you. I wish to live a life that is honoring to you. Protect me from physical, spiritual and emotional dangers. When I am weak, comfort me and give me strength. Make my body, mind and spirit healthy. I ask your blessings on all that I think, say and do. I ask the grace of a holy life and death. Amen.

Write Down Your Reflections and Feelings:

Chapter 32

I Am Getting Stronger & Healthier

People are always asking about my health and what the doctors are saying. I have decided that the best response is, *"I am getting stronger and healthier every day."*

Question: *"What does the doctor say?"*
Response: *"I am getting stronger and healthier every day."*

Question: *"How are you feeling?"*
Response: *"I am getting stronger and healthier every day."*

Word of God   Proverbs 10:11

The mouth of the just is a fountain of life.

Word of God   Proverbs 10:8(KJV)

The wise in heart will receive commandments: but a prating fool shall fall.

The tongue is a small member and yet has great pretensions ... We put bits into the mouths of horses to make them obey us, we also guide their whole bodies. It is the same with ships: even though they are so large and driven by fierce winds, they are steered by a very small rudder wherever the pilot's inclination wishes. In the same way the tongue is a small member ... [and] From the same mouth come blessing and cursing.

Prayer

Father God, thank you for this day and for this moment. Thank you for making me stronger and healthier every day. I receive your gift of physical, spiritual, and emotional healing. Please bless the words that I speak and protect my ears. I bind to myself today:

God's power to protect me,
God's strength to provide for me,
God's wisdom to guide me,
God's eyes to watch over me,
God's ear to hear my prayers,
God's hand to help me,
God's will to bless me,
God's love to secure me.
Amen.

Write Down Your Reflections and Feelings:

Chapter 33
The Battle Of Control
Continues

One day I possess faith in you Lord and you graciously give me peace. The next day I try to take back control and instantly peace leaves, and I feel anxious. Letting go and letting God is not a one-time event. Choosing to let you be God of me and my life is a choice I engage in moment by moment.

Word of God   Matthew 10:24(KJV)

The disciple is not above his master, nor the servant above his lord.

Word of God   1 Corinthians 3:7

Therefore, neither the one who plants nor the one who waters is anything, but only God, who causes the growth.

Word of God   Proverbs 3:6

In all your ways be mindful of him, and he will make straight your paths.

Prayer

Lord God, creator of heaven and earth, gently guide me on this journey where you are first in my life. I put into your hands my mind, heart, and soul. I give control to you, let me not be dismayed. Amen.

Write Down Your Reflections and Feelings:

Chapter 34

Do Not Worry About Your Life

The more I let go and let God, the better I feel. I am slowly seeing how "Do not worry lest you fall" and "I can do all things through Christ who strengthens me" manifests in my life. Learning to be obedient to God has meant giving up what previously made me feel secure and in control, but yet the more I let go and draw closer to God the better I feel.

Word of God   Jeremiah 17:7–8

Blessed are those who trust in the LORD; the LORD will be their trust. They are like a tree planted beside the waters that stretches out its roots to the stream: It does not fear heat when it comes, its leaves stay green; In the year of drought it shows no distress, but still produces fruit.

Word of God   2 Corinthians 1:3–4

Blessed be the God and Father of our LORD Jesus Christ, the Father of compassion and God of all encouragement, who encourages us in our every affliction, so that we may be able to encourage those who are in any affliction with the encouragement with which we ourselves are encouraged by God.

Word of God   Philippians 4:6–7

Have no anxiety at all, but in everything, by prayer and petition, with thanksgiving, make your requests known to God. Then the peace of God that surpasses all understanding will guard your hearts and minds in Christ Jesus.

Word of God   Matthew 6:25, 33–34

Therefore I tell you, do not worry about your life, what you will eat, or about your body, what you will wear ... But seek first the kingdom of God and his righteousness, and all these things will be given you besides. Do not worry about tomorrow; tomorrow will take care of itself. Sufficient for a day is its own evil.

Prayer

Gracious loving God, you are Lord of this day. You are Lord over all my senses. I thank you for this sense of peace and joy. You are Lord of my life. I receive the peace that can only come from you Lord, and I trust in your goodness. Thank you Father, Son, and Holy Spirit. Amen.

Write Down Your Reflections and Feelings:

Chapter 35

I Am Truly Blessed

Although I am experiencing a physical health challenge, I am truly blessed. I am blessed to have a wonderful family and friends. I am blessed to know God. I am blessed in countless ways. God has, and continues to faithfully provide.

Word of God   Romans 5:1–2, 5

We have peace with God through our LORD Jesus Christ, through whom we have gained access [by faith] to this grace in which we stand, and we boast in hope of the glory of God ... Because the love of God has been poured out into our hearts through the Holy Spirit that has been given to us.

Word of God   Galatians 5:22–23(ASV)

The fruit of the Spirit is love, joy, peace, longsuffering, kindness, goodness, faithfulness, meekness, self-control.

Word of God   Psalm 40:2–4

Surely, I wait for the LORD; who bends down to me and hears my cry, Draws me up from the pit of destruction ... Sets my feet upon rock, steadies my steps, And puts a new song in my mouth, a hymn to our God.

Prayer

Thank you God for drawing me to you. Thank you for opening my mind, eyes, and heart to all the blessings and gifts you have given me. It is through your grace that I now see and recognize all these blessings. Forgive me for being blind to these gifts and for the times I have neglected you. Thank you for the gift of Jesus and this gift of new life. Amen.

Write Down Your Blessings:

Chapter 36

Think Joyfully

My thoughts are powerful so I choose to control what I think. I now choose to think joyfully and when negative thoughts enter my mind I say "delete, delete, delete." And then repeat the statement, "I am totally and perfectly healthy," five times.

Word of God   Philippians 4:8

Whatever is true, whatever is honorable, whatever is just, whatever is pure, whatever is lovely, whatever is gracious, if there is any excellence and if there is anything worthy of praise, think about these things.

Word of God   Romans 5:1–5

Therefore, since we have been justified by faith, we have peace with God through our LORD Jesus Christ, through whom we have gained access [by faith] to this grace in which we stand, and we boast in hope of the glory of God. Not only that, but we even boast of our afflictions, knowing that affliction produces endurance, and endurance, proven character, and proven character, hope, and hope does not disappoint, because the love of God has been poured out into our hearts through the holy Spirit that has been given to us.

Therefore I tell you, all that you ask for in prayer, believe that you will receive it and it shall be yours. When you stand to pray, forgive anyone against whom you have a grievance, so that your heavenly Father may in turn forgive you your transgressions.

Prayer

Gracious God, my heart and mind are ready to burst with joy. I desire to dwell upon you, your goodness, and the blessings and gifts that I am grateful for. Let my joy shine forth from my words and actions to those I encounter. Amen.

Write Down Your Reflections and Feelings:

Chapter 37

God Made Me And Loves Me

The journey of cancer is difficult, but through this journey I have learned to love God, love myself, and truly love others. I thought I loved others before this journey began, but I see the love that I now experience as deeper and kinder. God's love pours through me.

Word of God   Sirach 42:15, 22–25

By the LORD's word his works were brought into being ... How beautiful are all his works, delightful to gaze upon and a joy to behold! Everything lives and abides forever; and to meet each need all things are preserved. All of them differ, one from another, yet none of them has he made in vain; For each in turn, as it comes, is good; can one ever see enough of their splendor?

Word of God   Jeremiah 31:3–4

With age-old love I have loved you; so I have kept my mercy toward you. Again I will build you, and you shall stay built.

Word of God   Psalm 139:13–14

You formed my inmost being; you knit me in my mother's womb. I praise you, because I am wonderfully made; wonderful are your works! My very self you know.

Prayer

Gracious loving Father, maker of heaven and earth, and of me, I am overcome with the thought that you made the earth, and with the same care and love you made me. This is truly an awesome thought. Thank you for loving me and being my Father. Thank you for not abandoning me when I neglected and abandoned you. Thank you for loving me even when I was unlovable. I love you and give myself to you, my Creator and Lord. Amen.

Write Down Your Reflections and Feelings:

Chapter 38

Believing Is Seeing

It is as if I have new eyes in which to see. I look around and see God's fingerprint everywhere. I see a world that was created perfectly and precisely. Trees that transform carbon dioxide into living oxygen for humans. The brilliant contrast of the white clouds and the blue sky. These items have surrounded me my whole life but now that I have changed internally, I now see God's presence in physical manifestations.

Word of God   Job 12:7–10

But now ask the beasts to teach you, the birds of the air to tell you; Or speak to the earth to instruct you, and the fish of the sea to inform you. Which of all these does not know that the hand of God has done this? In his hand is the soul of every living thing, and the life breath of all mortal flesh.

Word of God   Proverbs 3:19(KJV)

The LORD by wisdom hath founded the earth; by understanding hath he established the heavens.

Prayer

Thank you God for removing the scales from my eyes, and showing me what has been around me all my life. Lord, I ask to live according to your will, and trust you are working through this illness to heal me physically, spiritually, and emotionally. Thank you for the miracle of this life. I praise you and the works of your hand. Amen.

Write Down Your Reflections and Feelings:

Chapter 39

Always Remember Who You Belong To

This journey is hard, but as I look back I see that every step of it was needed in order to shed the old to make room for the Lord and for what is new, clean, and wholesome. It is clear that I was living to glorify myself and the world as opposed to remembering that I belong to the Lord and should live to glorify God.

Word of God   Isaiah 49:15

Can a mother forget her infant, be without tenderness for the child of her womb? Even should she forget, I will never forget you.

Word of God   Psalm 24:1

The earth is the LORD's and all it holds, the world and those who dwell in it.

Word of God   Romans 12:12

Rejoice in hope, endure in affliction, persevere in prayer.

*e*veryone **who listens** to these words of mine and acts on them will be like a wise man who built his house on rock. The rain fell, the floods came, and the winds blew and buffeted the house. But it did not collapse; it had been set solidly on rock.

Prayer

Most blessed Trinity, with all of my heart I thank you for your mercy. My heart desires to know you and serve you. My eyes have been opened and I see what previously was hidden from my sight. You carried me when I could not carry myself. You gave me strength when I was weak. You carried my sins and forgave my transgressions. Thank you for the gift of loving myself. Glory be to the Father, the Son, and the Holy Spirit, as it was in the beginning, is now, and forever will be. Amen.

Write Down Your Reflections and Feelings:

Chapter 40

Forgiving Myself

Lord I know you are gracious and kind and that you have forgiven me. I now need to fully forgive myself and my past. I am no longer the person I used to be. It is time for me to release the past and the painful experiences that have haunted me.

Word of God   Isaiah 43:25

It is I, I, who wipe out ... your offenses; your sins I remember no more.

Word of God   Isaiah 43:18–19

Remember not the events of the past, the things of long ago consider not; see, I am doing something new! Now it springs forth, do you not perceive it?

Word of God   Galatians 4:7

So you are no longer a slave but a child, and if a child then also an heir, through God.

With age-old love I have loved you; so I have kept my mercy toward you. Again I will build you, and you shall stay built.

Prayer

Father, it is so clear to me now that you will use my actions toward others as a measuring stick for judging me. You will forgive me according to how I have forgiven others, including myself. God, I forgive myself for every silly, selfish, rude, self-serving and unkind word, action and thought. I forgive myself fully and completely. The past is over and I am free. I choose to forgive myself and love myself. Thank you God for this grace. Amen.

Write Down Your Reflections and Feelings:

Chapter 41

Fear Is Subsiding And
Joy Is Taking Root

A comforting peace has embraced me and assures me that I am safe. I still pray for life and perfect health, but because I know God, the creator of the universe loves me, I feel a new love for myself and the world he created. This glimpse into the grand design God created for us is awesome and fills me with joy. I feel a warmth and lightness that did not exist previously.

A Word from God

Precious little one, there is no fear in love because love casts out all fear. Do not worry about the future or what you will wear for I will provide for you. There are no more things from which you can run, for I shall always be with you. Do not worry lest you fail. I am one with you and you shall not suffer. The suffering is done now so you shall live. Your life is a tribute to all that is good and worthy. Your love and light are a tribute to me. I will forever guide you so that you can make me shine.

Word of God   Psalm 34:4(KJV)

I sought the LORD, and he heard me, and delivered me from all my fears.

Word of God   Isaiah 40:31

They that hope in the LORD will renew their strength, they will soar as with eagles' wings; They will run and not grow weary, walk and not grow faint.

Word of God   Isaiah 41:10

Do not fear: I am with you; do not be anxious: I am your God. I will strengthen you, I will help you, I will uphold you with my victorious right hand.

Word of God   Isaiah 54:10

Though the mountains fall away and the hills be shaken, My love shall never fall away from you nor my covenant of peace be shaken, says the LORD.

Prayer

Gracious and loving Jesus, thank you for being my Lord, God, and Savior. Thank you for the gift of loving myself. Please baptize me anew in your Holy Spirit of love, joy, peace, truth, and perfect health this day and every day. I ask this in the name of Jesus and through the immaculate heart of my loving Mother Mary. Amen.

Write Down Your Reflections and Feelings:

Chapter 42

Moving Forward Step By Step

This illness is a journey in which I have been both a passenger and driver. I am a passenger in the sense of the physical illness itself and that I did not knowingly ask to go on the journey of cancer. I am a driver in the sense that I am choosing whether to actively participate and move forward step by step in the emotional and spiritual healing opportunities that this journey has offered.

Word of God   Psalm 71:1–7

In you, LORD, I take refuge; let me never be put to shame. In your justice rescue and deliver me; listen to me and save me! Be my rock of refuge, my stronghold to give me safety; for you are my rock and fortress. My God, rescue me from the hand of the wicked, from the clutches of the evil and violent. You are my hope, LORD; my trust, GOD, ... my hope in you never wavers. I have become a portent to many, but you are my strong refuge!

Word of God   Isaiah 42:16

I will lead the blind on a way they do not know; by paths they do not know I will guide them. I will turn darkness into light before them, and make crooked ways straight. These are my promises: I made them, I will not forsake them.

*Y*ou saw how the LORD, your God, carried you, as one carries his own child, all along your journey until you arrived at this place.

Prayer

Father, Son, and Holy Spirit, please bless each step of this journey: the medicine, the doctors, the nurses, and my family and friends. Please continue to carry and guide me on this journey. Father God, you know all things so you know that it is my deepest desire to be healed physically, emotionally, and spiritually. Please lead me and heal me. I ask this in Jesus' name and through the immaculate heart of my Mother Mary. Amen.

Write Down Your Reflections and Feelings:

Chapter 43

Begin Anew

I now understand that energy begets energy and if I dwell upon the negative it grows. Conversely, if I dwell upon the positive it grows. I no longer want to dwell upon negative situations or people that I have been hurt by or that I have hurt. I am ready to begin anew.

Word of God   Ephesians 4:26–27, 29–31

*D*o not let the sun set on your anger, and do not leave room for the devil. No foul language should come out of your mouths, but only such as is good for needed edification, that it may impart grace to those who hear. And do not grieve the holy Spirit of God, with which you were sealed for the day of redemption. All bitterness, fury, anger, shouting, and reviling must be removed from you, along with all malice.

Word of God   Psalm 37:8–9

*R*efrain from anger; abandon wrath; do not be provoked; it brings only harm. Those who do evil will be cut off, but those who wait for the LORD will inherit the earth.

Word of God   Matthew 5:22

*W*hoever is angry with his brother will be liable to judgment.

Whatever is true, whatever is honorable, whatever is just, whatever is pure, whatever is lovely, whatever is gracious, if there is any excellence and if there is anything worthy of praise, think about these things.

Prayer

Dearest Jesus, my Lord and my God, please ask the Holy Spirit to go back into my memory and heal every hurt and pain that has ever been done to me. Please heal every hurt and pain that I have ever caused to another person. I pray for restoration for those individuals.

Please heal all the relationships that have been damaged in my whole life, especially where there is hurt that I am not aware of. Lord if someone is suffering from my hand or words, then please bring to my attention that person. I choose to forgive and I ask to be forgiven.

Remove any bitterness, hatred, anger, resentment or unforgiveness that exists in me and fill all those empty spaces with Jesus' pure perfect love. I now lovingly release and let go of the past and all past experiences. The past is over and I am free. I ask for these intentions in Jesus' name and through the immaculate heart of my Mother Mary. Amen.

Write Down Your Reflections and Feelings:

Chapter 44

I'll Do It Your Way Lord

I desire to live <u>in</u> the world, but not be <u>of</u> the world. I desire to live according to God's decrees because I know that it leads to life and joy. For decades I lived according to my rules. I lived my way and it does not work. I want to live your way Lord.

A Word from God

This day I will bring glory to all that know and trust in Jesus Christ. Do not be afraid for I am with you always. Your life and love are in me forever.

Word of God   1 Corinthians 2:12

We have not received the spirit of the world but the Spirit that is from God, so that we may understand the things freely given us by God.

Word of God   Psalm 119:129–130

Wonderful are your testimonies; therefore I keep them. The revelation of your words sheds light, gives understanding to the simple.

Word of God   2 Corinthians 5:14–15

The love of Christ impels us ... so that those who live might no longer live for themselves but for him who for their sake died and was raised.

Word of God   Psalm 19:8, 10, 12, 15

The law of the LORD is perfect, refreshing the soul. The decree of the LORD is trustworthy, giving wisdom to the simple ... The statutes of the LORD are true, all of them just; By them your servant is warned; obeying them brings much reward. Let the words of my mouth be acceptable, the thoughts of my heart before you, LORD, my rock and my redeemer.

Word of God   Jeremiah 42:3

Let the LORD God show us what way we should take and what we should do.

Prayer

Lord Jesus Christ, you know me through and through and still choose to love me. My deepest and darkest emotions and thoughts are as clear as the page of a book lying open in the sunlight to you.

Today I choose to consecrate myself to you rather than hide from you. I place my life in your hands. I consecrate to you my body, my soul and all that I am. I ask you to guard and guide all my thoughts, words and deeds, all my sufferings and labors, all my hopes, consolations, and joys.

I place my trust in you without reserve. I pray for the remission of my sins through your grace and mercy. Your loving hands have fashioned me and I now place all my cares and anxieties in those same hands. Jesus, I now allow you to lead me in this journey of life. Do with me what you will. Amen.

Write Down Your Reflections and Feelings:

Chapter 45

I Am Not Who I Was

This journey has been long and painful. Although I would never desire to go through it again, I now see why God did not miraculously heal me. I am not the same person I was at the beginning of this journey.

Word of God   John 15:1–2

I am the true vine, and my Father is the vine grower. He takes away every branch in me that does not bear fruit, and every one that does he prunes so that it bears more fruit.

Word of God   Hebrews 12:10–11

They disciplined us for a short time as seemed right to them, but he does so for our benefit, in order that we may share his holiness. At the time, all discipline seems a cause not for joy but for pain, yet later it brings the peaceful fruit of righteousness to those who are trained by it.

Word of God   Romans 8:28

We know that all things work for good for those who love God, who are called according to his purpose.

Prayer

Father, Son, and Holy Spirit, I bless you and praise you for your mercy and wisdom. I started this journey thinking I was a good person but my eyes have been opened. I now see how sinful and prideful I was. Through your grace and tenderness Lord, I am no longer the same person I was. I am a new creation in you. Bless you, Father, Son, and Holy Spirit. Amen.

Write Down Your Reflections and Feelings:

Chapter 46

A Life That Glorifies God

I am not who I was before cancer. I am physically different in that I look different. I am emotionally different because anger, guilt, and shame have been replaced with peace, love, and joy. I am spiritually different in that I now know Jesus personally. I seek to live a life that honors and glorifies Jesus. I seek to live according to God's will and not my own desires.

Word of God   Tobit 4:5–6

Perform **righteous deeds** all the days of your life, and do not tread the paths of wickedness. For those who act with fidelity, all who practice righteousness, will prosper in their affairs.

Word of God   Colossians 3:17(KJV)

Whatsoever ye do in word or deed, do all in the name of the LORD Jesus, giving thanks to God and the Father by him.

Word of God   Romans 2:7

Eternal life to those who seek glory, honor, and immortality through perseverance in good works.

Prayer

My Blessed Trinity, Father, Son, and Holy Spirit. I wish for my life through word, thought, and deed, to glorify you and honor you. When I drift into living of the world please gently remind me of my promise and desire to live a life that glorifies you. Thank you for your mercies. Amen.

Write Down Your Reflections and Feelings:

Appendix

Prayers and Novenas

JESUS' LOVING AND SACRED HEART

Dear Sacred and Loving Heart of Jesus, grant me the grace of health in body, mind, and spirit so I may serve you with strength. Gently touch me so that I may serve you with strength this day and forever. Amen.

BLESSING PRAYER

Dear ever loving and generous God, you are with me always. Let your power protect me. Let your eyes watch over me. Let your love fill me. Let your goodness embody me. Amen.

PRAYER TO THE SACRED HEART OF JESUS

Oh Sacred Heart of Jesus, filled with infinite love, broken by my ingratitude, pierced by my sins, and yet, loving me still, relying on thy promise of infinite charity when you said, "Come to me all you that labor and are burdened and I will refresh you."

I Come to thee and in the lowliness of my heart earnestly beg thee to grant me your loving help. Amen.

Prayer to the Sacred Heart of Jesus
Reprinted by permission from the Reed Candle Company
www.reedcandlecompany.com

MARY, MY MOTHER PRAYER

Ever Virgin Mary, Mother of Mercy, Health of the Sick, Comforter of the Afflicted, you know my hopes, dreams, and sufferings; grant me mercy and health through your loving Son, Jesus.

In Lourdes, France you appeared to St. Bernadette and spoke of dispensing your favors. I come before you now, confident, and implore your intercession to obtain on this day, spiritual, physical and emotional healing for (mention person's name).

Loving mother of Jesus and my Mother, please obtain these mercies and graces for (mention person's name). I wish to live a life that imitates your virtues while you were on Earth.

Thank you Mother and I pray this in the name of Jesus and through your most immaculate heart. Amen.

PRAYER TO OUR LADY OF THE
MIRACULOUS MEDAL

Virgin Mother of God, Mary Immaculate,
we unite ourselves to you under your title of
Our Lady of the Miraculous Medal.

May this medal be for each one of us
a sure sign of your motherly affection for us and a
constant reminder of our filial duties towards you.

While wearing it, may we be blessed by your loving
protection and preserved in the grace of your Son.
Most powerful Virgin, Mother of our Savior, keep us close to
you every moment of our lives so that like you we may live and
act according to the teaching and example of your Son.

Obtain for us, your children, the grace of a happy death
so that in union with you we may enjoy
the happiness of heaven forever.

Amen.

O Mary, conceived without sin, pray for us who have recourse to you.

Reprinted by Permission from The Association of the Miraculous Medal
An apostolate of the Congregation of the Mission Western Province
www.amm.org

PRAYER TO SAINT JOSEPH

O Saint Joseph whose protection is so great, so strong, so prompt before the Throne of God, I place in you all my interests and desires. O Saint Joseph do assist me by your powerful intercession and obtain for me from your Divine Son all spiritual blessings through Jesus Christ, Our Lord; so that having engaged here below your Heavenly power, I may offer my Thanksgiving and Homage to the most Loving of Fathers.

O Saint Joseph, I never weary of contemplating you and Jesus asleep in your arms. I dare not approach while he reposes near your heart. Press him in my name and kiss his fine head for me, and ask Him to return the Kiss when I draw my dying breath. Saint Joseph, Patron of departing souls, pray for us. Amen.

Say for nine consecutive mornings for anything you may desire. It has seldom been known to fail.

This prayer was found in the fiftieth year of Our Lord Jesus Christ. In 1500's it was sent by the Pope to Emperor Charles when he was going into battle.

Whoever reads this prayer or hear it or carries it, will never die a sudden death, nor be drowned, nor will poison take effect on them. They will not fall into the hands of the enemy nor be burned in any fire, nor will they be defeated in battle.

Prayer to Saint Joseph
Reprinted with permission from The Pieta Prayer Book
© MLOR Corporation 2003

PRAYER TO SAINT THERESE OF
LISIEUX, THE LITTLE FLOWER OF JESUS

Saint Therese, precious Little Flower of Jesus, I graciously ask for your intercession as I stand in great need of physical and spiritual healing. Please pray for me and I beg you to bring my most urgent petitions, especially (mention your requests) to our holy and divine Savior, Jesus Christ.

As a sign of your kind intercession, I humbly ask that you shower me with your promised roses of virtue and grace. Thank you for your wondrous example of devotion and dedication to our most Blessed Lord, and I pray I may someday receive the crown of life, which our Lord Jesus Christ has promised to those who love him. Amen.

NOVENA TO SAINT THERESE
OF THE CHILD JESUS

Saint Therese, the Little Flower,
Please pick me a rose from the Heavenly Garden
And send it to me with a message of Love
Ask God to grant me the favor I Thee implore
And tell Him I will love Him each day more and more.

Novena to Saint Therese of the Child Jesus
Reprinted with permission from The Pieta Prayer Book
© MLOR Corporation 2003

PRAYER FOR A MIRACLE

Lord Jesus Christ, Almighty Son of God, I humbly come before you and ask you to please forgive me of all my sins and transgressions. I love you and I never want to be separated from you. Help me to forgive in my heart, those who have injured me. I reject and renounce Satan, who is the father of lies and the deceiver of the whole world, all the evil spirits and fallen angels, and their evil works.

Lord Jesus Christ, you are the Light of the World, the Good Shepherd, and to you I give my entire self – all my thoughts, all my words, and all my actions. I accept you as my Lord, God and Savior, and ask that you strengthen and heal me in body, soul, and spirit.

I pray, Lord Jesus, that you cover me with your precious blood and send your holy Angels to surround and protect me. Fill me with the gift of the Holy Spirit. Lord, God, I love you above all things and rely on the help of your grace for strength, wisdom, and courage to follow you faithfully every day of my life.

Holy Mary, Mother of Our Redeemer, Saint Jude, patron of desperate cases, Saint Peregrine, patron for those suffering from cancer, and all of God's Angels and Saints, I seek your intercession for healing and comfort.

Amen.

NOVENA TO OUR LADY OF GUADALUPE

Our Lady of Guadalupe, according to your message in Mexico I venerate you as "the Virgin Mother of the true God for whom we live, the Creator of all the world, maker of heaven and earth." In spirit I kneel before your most Holy Image which you miraculously imprinted upon the cloak of the Indian Juan Diego, and with the faith of the countless numbers of pilgrims who visit your shrine, I beg you for this favor (mention your request).

Remember, O Immaculate Virgin, the words you spoke to your devout client, "I am a merciful Mother to you and to all your people who love me and trust in me and invoke my help. I listen to their lamentations and solace all their sorrows and their sufferings." I beg you to be a merciful Mother to me, because I sincerely love you and trust in you and invoke your help. I entreat you, Our Lady of Guadalupe, to grant my request, if this should be the Will of God, in order that I may "Bear witness to your love, your compassion, your help and protection." Do not forsake me in my needs. Our Lady of Guadalupe, pray for us.

Hail Mary (3 times)

PRAYER TO SAINT JUDE THADDEUS

But you, beloved, build yourselves up in your most holy faith;
pray in the Holy Spirit.
Keep yourselves in the love of God
and wait for the mercy of our Lord Jesus Christ.
Jude 1:20–21

Blessed Saint Jude Thaddeus, devoted servant and follower of Jesus Christ, you faithfully preached the Gospel with great passion, often in the most difficult situations, and as a result through the power of the Holy Spirit, you made a profound difference in the lives of many people.

Saint Jude Thaddeus, when you preached the Gospel, you stressed how the faithful should persevere in times of great difficulties, and to stand firm in the power of God who protects us and keeps us from falling. Dearest Saint Jude Thaddeus, I ask for your prayers as I am losing the strength to pray as I should. Pray for me as my courage is faltering, and I am growing weary and unable to find relief. I ask for your powerful intercession before Jesus Christ, for all my trials and sufferings, particularly (mention your request).

Obtain for me the grace from God to accept these trials with faith, patience, and strength. If it's God's will, grant that I be delivered from my suffering and restore me to health.

I will forever praise and honor my Savior, Jesus Christ, Mary, Mother of Good Counsel, my special and powerful patron, Saint Jude Thaddeus, and all of God's Angels and Saints.

Amen.

PRAYER TO SAINT JUDE

O Holy Saint Jude you are great in virtue and rich in miracles. While on Earth you were one of the twelve Apostles and often referred to as Thaddeus, which means "amiable" or "loving." The Church honors and invokes you universally as the Patron Saint of hopeless cases--of things despaired of. You, Saint Jude, are the Patron Saint of the impossible and desperate. Pray for me as I come to you confidently and implore your aid.

Be my loving intercessor and special patron in this time of great need. Intercede on my behalf with God for visible and speedy help where help is almost despaired of. From the depths of my heart I humbly ask you, Saint Jude, to grant my earnest petition of (mention your request). Saint Jude, graciously help me in this time of urgent need, and I will never forget the graces and favors you obtain for me. I promise, O blessed Saint Jude, to be ever mindful of this great favor granted me by God and to always honor you as my most special patron and to graciously let others know of my devotion to you. Amen.

May the Most Sacred Heart of Jesus be adored and loved in all the tabernacles until the end of time. Amen.

May the most Sacred Heart of Jesus be praised and glorified now and forever. Amen

Saint Jude pray for us and hear our prayers. Amen.

Blessed be the Sacred Heart of Jesus.
Blessed be the Immaculate Heart of Mary.
Blessed be Saint Jude Thaddeus, in all the world and for all Eternity.

Saint Jude, pray for us and all who honor thee and invoke thy aid.

(Say 3 Our Father's, 3 Hail Mary's, and 3 Glory Be's after this.)

In addition to your prayer petition to Saint Jude, his aid can be invoked by:

- Offering Holy Mass and lifting up Communion in his honor.
- Leaving 9 copies of this prayer in church, 9 consecutive days as a Novena.
- Performing charitable works in honor of Saint Jude. (Saint Leo commented "Prayer has the greatest efficacy to obtain favors from God when it is supported by works of mercy.")

PRAYER TO SAINT PEREGRINE

Dear Saint Peregrine, you are often called "Wonder Worker" because of the countless miracles in which you have so kindly obtained from God. Saint Peregrine, during your life on earth you traveled the journey of cancer and through the grace of God you were miraculously healed the eve before you were to have surgery.

I come to you confidently and implore your aid with God in my necessity. Saint Peregrine, please pray for me to the Lord our God for my physical, spiritual, and emotional healing, specifically I pray for (mention your request).

Have mercy on me Saint Peregrine, God the Father, God the Son, and sweet Holy Spirit. With confidence and thanksgiving I will sing to God, now and forever, a song of gratitude for this great mercy. Please grant this favor for which I now petition. Bless you Saint Peregrine and most holy Trinity. Amen.

Saint Peregrine, pray for me
And for all who invoke your aid.
(repeat 3 times)

Afterword

It is my hope that you found this devotional helpful and encouraging. My personal journey to Christ continues to be a lifelong journey. I am grateful to God for graciously sharing his love with me when I was so unworthy of it.

I pray that you will seek God in whatever difficulty you are facing. He desires you, and through his amazing grace he will give you the strength you need to deal with that difficulty and be victorious.

May the Lord bless you and keep you.
S. Jude Peregrine

Scripture Index

Scripture Index

About The Author

Today my life is joyous and rich. I have a wonderful husband who is a hottie, fun, and truly loving. I have two children that are teenagers. I wake up every morning in a good mood and see all the joy and good things in my life. I have a great job that is challenging and connects me with a lot people. I feel terrific and energized! Today I see and feel my life is truly awesome, and I am thankful to Jesus Christ for the amazing gift of life.

In 2002 my life was quite different. From all outward appearances many would say that my life looked similar to what my life looks like now. I had the same hottie husband, a thriving career where I was making more money than I ever imagined, a beautiful house, and a wonderful family. Yes, from the outside much was the same, but internally my life was as different as day is to night. Although I would not have said it at the time, my life was missing joy. My calendar was full of activities, vacations, shopping; but they were truly meaningless in their pursuit.

What changed? My health. At age 38, I was diagnosed with a rare form of cancer, and that is really where my story begins.

Like many people who find out they are ill, I went through the standard medical procedure of chemotherapy, surgery, more chemotherapy, and radiation. It was a yearlong journey. A journey that I would wish upon no one, but a journey I now understand and am thankful that I went through. It seems strange to think how someone could be thankful for losing their hair and their breasts. But I am. It is only because of that enormous struggle that I now have wonderful joy. Because of that journey, I was healed physically, emotionally, and spiritually. Prior to being diagnosed with cancer, I had no clue how ill I was emotionally and spiritually. After being diagnosed with Stage 3B cancer, I kept thinking, "How could God let this happen to me – is he punishing me? I go to church every Sunday." What I know now is that God was not punishing me. He was, however, trying to get my attention.

Up to that point in my life I could analyze, navigate, and fix almost any challenge I faced. But stage 3B breast cancer was something I could not fix. That challenge was beyond me. Although the statistics were not encouraging, I felt optimistic; A grace from God. And so my journey began. I began by going through test after test, and doctor visit after doctor visit.

At the same time I was diagnosed with cancer, my husband lost his job. His company was acquired and they did not need two CFOs. But God provided. He provided my husband with a new job. Out of the blue, a former employer called and offered my husband a job which he was not qualified for, had no experience in, and at a 40% pay cut. However, it was enough at the time to sustain our family. This was one of my first glimpses of God from a different perspective. God continued to provide for my needs.

When I was initially diagnosed I thought I would work throughout my treatments. After all, work was a big part of my life and at the time one of the main reasons I existed. Clue 1 as to how ill I was spiritually and emotionally. Well, after a few weeks of trying to juggle a demanding job, doctor appointments and tests, I realized I could not work at the pace required that made my employer so successful. So, tearfully, I wrote my resignation letter and submitted it to my boss and the owner of the company. The owner of the company instructed my boss to pay me the difference between disability and my salary; A gift from God. He also instructed the benefits coordinator to work with the company's health insurance provider to make sure all of my medical bills were covered as much as possible; Another gift from God.

At home, in the mornings, after my husband left for work and my children left for school, I suddenly found myself alone with time that was unplanned and unoccupied. Two thoughts crossed my mind with what to do with this new found time: *I can clean the house or I can go to Mass.*

I actually did not know daily Mass even existed until a week before resigning from my job. Clue 2 how ill I was spiritually. I remember standing in front of the large beveled mirror in my white shiny master bathroom and thinking, "Well, I don't have anything better to do so I might as well go to Mass." It sounds so funny when I reflect on this now. I now believe that this choice of going to Mass that day was monumentally significant to my healing, physically and spiritually.

And so I went to Mass. To my surprise, the chapel was crowded. How strange it seemed that people who were healthy went to Mass on week days.

After I was diagnosed, I met with my priest. I was still so confused why God let this happen to me. I saw God at that time like a parent that rewards and punishes based on behavior. My priest did not have answers but he did expose me to the concept that God loved me and how God even knows how many hairs there are on my head. I didn't fully understand this God and prayed that God would heal me miraculously.

During this same visit my priest asked me about the last time I went to confession. At the time I was a Catholic who did not practice the basics of my faith. Just as I had contemplated in my bathroom about going to Mass, I clearly remember sitting across from the priest in his office, surrounded by all the books on the shelves contemplating his question about confession. I was thinking about why would I need to go to confession when I was a good person; I didn't kill or steal or commit adultery or... "But what the heck, I will go to confession." God's grace.

So I confessed things that in my mind did not break the Ten Commandments, because I thought I was good. I did however, confess things that bothered me. This confession was my first step to spiritual, emotional, and physical healing. This confession opened up something inside me and I started to cry. I did not understand, these items were not big. They were not breaking the commandments. I left that meeting with my priest feeling better, lighter.

Over the next 12 months I would continue to go to confession on a weekly basis. Things would bubble up and I would confess them accompanied by a stream of tears. Week after week, bit by bit, all of the spiritual and emotional hurts and pains made their way out. This was part of my journey and it juxtaposed my medical treatments. Every week for one year I would cry through every confession until one day I didn't. Finally, all those years of built up hurts and pains were fully washed away.

I am convinced that my physical healing was tied to my spiritual and emotional healing, and that reconciliation was the pathway to achieving health.

After I was healed and my life was relatively normal again, the Lord kept placing the thought of this book in my mind and that is how this devotional journal came to be. I hope this book is a gift to you.

Pen Name S. Jude Peregrine

This devotional was written under the pen name of S. Jude Peregrine to honor two of my favorite Patron Saints; Saint Jude Thaddeus and Saint Peregrine.

Saint Jude Thaddeus is the Patron Saint of lost causes and desperate cases. He preached the Gospel to Christians who at the time were being persecuted; he encouraged them to persevere during the difficult times and to keep their faith and love for God.

Saint Peregrine is the Patron Saint for people suffering with cancer. During his life, Saint Peregrine was often called the "Angel of Good Counsel." After being ordained a priest, Saint Peregrine went to Forli to found a Servite monastery. A few years later a cancerous growth appeared on his right foot. It was so painful that he finally agreed with the surgeon who wanted to amputate.

The night before the scheduled surgery, Saint Peregrine spent hours in prayer. Then he dozed off and dreamt that Christ was touching him and healing his foot. The thrill of it woke him up. In the dim moonlight he saw that his foot, carefully bandaged a few hours earlier was completely healed.

Both of these Saints were companions to me during my journey from cancer to Christ. Therefore, I humbly use the combination of their two names as the pen name for this book as a way of recognizing and honoring them.

Printed in the United States
By Bookmasters